THE TALE OF AN INFANT CRIMINAL!

The story of how a one-year-old baby broke the law and became a criminal.

By Peter Chase Wetherill

Text copyright c 2020 by Peter Chase Wetherill. All Rights Reserved. No part of this book may be used or reproduced in any matter whatsoever without the expressed written permission of the publisher.

Address all inquiries to: Peter Chase Wetherill, peterwetherill@hotmail.com.

DEDICATION

Thanks to my parents who were such an inspiration throughout my life.

ACKNOWLEDGMENTS

Thanks to my cousins, Price Wetherill and Wendy Wetherill, for finding family papers after cleaning out their father's garage, and sending them to me. Writer and publisher Ethan Casey, along with my cousin Carl Eschweiler for their research on the Hopkins family and their cooperation with me on research for this book. George Marshal for his research on the Denver properties and Denver family members. Writer D. Flodin Soderman for her research, and publishing "Emma Eliza Bucknell: Titanic Survivor". Special thanks go to my cousin Alleen-Marie Coke and her daughter for research, English language expertise, proof reading, and editing advice. Thanks to librarian Alex from the main branch of the Denver Public Library for finding archived Denver newspaper articles.

Cover design by Peter Chase Wetherill. Cover photo image from Wetherill family collection, all rights reserved. Image is of the US green card of Frank Loyson-Doster.

FORWARD

This is the story of how my father, Frank Doster Wetherill, came into the world and the problems he had immigrating to the US and becoming a US citizen. The process is familiar to many who enter the US from another country and have the desire to become US citizens. My father's story is not typical of the millions of people that enter the US. Becoming a US citizen was complicated for him even though he came from a well-connected family. Most people wishing to enter and stay permanently in the US have a more difficult time than my father did. This is the story of how his family circumstances caused his legal situation and how the immigration laws, at that time, made the solution complicated.

There are many different ways people enter the United States from other countries, both with and without documentation, and various paths for obtaining a US citizenship. Some become US citizens through marriage to a US citizen, as my mother did in the 1950s. This is called naturalization, and it is a common way for many to become citizens, others gain automatic citizenship if born in the US or its territories and are eligible for citizenship through naturalization if they have five years as a permanent resident, three years as a permanent resident and married to a US citizen for three years (my mother's example), or have qualifying service in the US armed services.

Another way, but not as common, is citizenship through acquisition. This is when a child is born overseas and automatically acquires a US citizenship. The child must have parents that are US citizens and at least one or both of them lived in the US or its territories before the birth, or one parent was a US citizen at the time of the child's birth, and the child was born on or after November 14, 1986, and the parents were married at the time of birth, and the US citizen parent was physically present in the US or its territories for a period of at least five years at some time in his or her life prior to the birth, of which at least two years were after his or her 14th birthday, or one parent was a US citizen at the time of the child's birth, and the birth date is before November 14, 1986, but after October 10, 1952, and the child's parents were married at the time of the birth, and the US citizen parent was physically present in the US or its territories for a period of at least ten years at some time in his or her life prior to the child's birth, at least five of which were after his or her 14th birthday. Simple enough isn't it?

One more way, that is constantly being challenged in the courts, is citizenship through derivation. When a parent naturalizes, his or her children (under the age of 18 and living with the parent at the time) may "derive" US citizenship automatically, provided they are also permanent residents. What is more, a child who gets US citizenship through derivation does not have to participate in a naturalization ceremony. Generally, foreign-born children under 18 automatically acquire US citizenship if three requirements are met: The child must have US lawful permanent resident status ("green card" holder); and at least one parent must be a US citizen; and the child must be residing in the United States in the legal and physical custody of a US citizen parent. (This information on citizenship taken from the web site updated on September 14, 2018:

https://citizenpath.com/ways-to-become-a-us-citizen/.)

Most pathways to becoming a US citizen depend on being a permanent legal resident. This entails obtaining a renewable "green card" through family, employment, special immigrant status, refugee or asylee status, human trafficking or crime victims, victims of abuse, and various others. Most people have heard of the Diversity Immigrant Lottery Program, (AKA the Green Card Lottery), which each year makes 50,000 immigrant visas available to countries with low immigration rates. More information is found on this web site:

https://www.usa.gov/green-cards.

As of 2020 there are 85.7 million immigrants and their children living in the US, and somewhere between 10 to 11.4 million people living in the US are undocumented, meaning they do not have green cards or temporary visas, (educational, work, or medical visas etc.). The reason this amount is not certain is that most undocumented persons do not want to be recognized because of the fear of deportation. The amount of documented and undocumented entries varies every year and has many different circumstances, as I mentioned before, for permanent legal entry. Many people are allowed to stay 90 days on a regular passport depending on the country of origin. There are three types of non-immigrant tourist visas: B1 visas (for business), B2 visas (for tourism or medical treatment), and combination B1/B2 visas when the reasons for visiting are business and tourism (and/or medical treatment). If a person overstays these visas it is not a federal crime, but a civil violation that is handled by immigration court proceedings.

Every year many people become undocumented immigrants after entering with and without documentation from countries all over the world. In 2016 there were 1.8 million legal immigrants who entered the US. About 44 million US residents were born in a foreign country, the highest percentage in the world. Both of my parents were foreign-born. In 2017, 600,000 people became undocumented by overstaying their visas and about 500,000 entered the US without documentation. These statistics vary every year, are not exact, are disputed, and vary, depending, on the source of reporting.

My father's story of how he became a US citizen is an example of this process, but takes place in the 1930s when rules were different. I will not list all the differences, because then this book would turn into a history of US immigration. Many of the rules from that time are still the same, such as a need for getting a "green card" to stay in the country legally. The main law that governed immigration at that time was The Immigration Act of 1924 (the Johnson-Reed Act). This act put strict quotas on immigration and forbade entry from most Asian countries. Japan was especially upset over this, which damaged Japanese/US relations, and you know what that led to!

The business leaders and politicians in the US who are anti-immigration often vilify undocumented immigrants as genetically inferior, rapists, murderers, criminals, drug dealers, addicts, disease-ridden, terrorists, or stealing jobs from US citizens. This is eugenic propaganda and has no statistical proof whatsoever. In fact the opposite is true. My parents are only one example. My father entered the US legally, became undocumented and then became a US citizen, and my mother entered the US legally, and then became a US citizen. Most US citizens can trace their roots back to immigrants. Even the Native Americans have Asian roots; their ancestors having migrated to the Americas thousands of years ago. The people of the US and all of North, Central, and South America have immigrant roots, and they have made all of the Americas stronger and more prosperous.

Maybe, it is human nature, to explore the unknown, to escape danger to protect themselves and their families, to join family members who are separated from them, to live in freedom, to seek riches, or just to try to find a better life. This is the main reason for migration, not to go to the US to commit crimes and be involved in criminal behavior, or escape prosecution in their home countries, as many racists and politicians would like people to believe.

I hope you enjoy this story. Even if you don't agree with my view on immigration, accept that not all immigrants are the same, just like not all people are the same, and people should not be judged by what they are but by who they are.

This book could actually be considered the last book chronologically of a multi book series about my unusual family. The first was an autobiography written by my great-great-grandmother, which I will mention later, which I edited and published in 2019. I would love to hear any comments on this book, and any well written reviews would be appreciated. Please subscribe to any or all of my social media or my Amazon author page for special offers and new releases. Here are my social media contacts:

For photos, this is the Frank Doster Wetherill Facebook Page:

https://www.facebook.com/Frank-Doster-Wetherill-346352446482259

Blog: https://peterwetherill.com/

Facebook:
https://www.facebook.com/peter.wetherill/

Twitter: @peterwetherill

Instagram:
https://www.instagram.com/peterchasewetherill/

Amazon Author Page: Peter Chase Wetherill

TABLE OF CONTENTS

Dedication iii
Acknowledgments iv
Forward v
Chapter 1. The Family of My Father's Mother 1
Chapter 2. My Father's Father's Family 16
Chapter 3. How My Grandparents Met 23
Chapter 4. Marriage, Divorce, and the Birth of My Father 33
Chapter 5. Breaking the Law and Becoming a Legal Resident of the US 39
Post log 53

CHAPTER 1

The Family of My Father's Mother

The family of my father's mother contains prominent names such as Doster, Gumaer, Nichols, Bidwell, Hill, Barnum, and Taylor, all of which were influential in Colorado, some internationally known, and all of them well-to-do. Some are even familiar today and important in US history.

My father's mother, Dorothy Doster, was born in Denver, Colorado on July 10, 1910, and died in 1986. She came from a wealthy Denver family. Her father, Chase Doster (1873-1935), was a West Point graduate and career military man. He achieved the rank of Colonel and served with many generals, the most famous of which was General Pershing. He served in many wars and was a member of the first US unit to arrive in Europe in WWI. He contracted malaria while serving in the Philippines, which later led to his early retirement, frequent hospital stays, and an early death at 62 years of age. My middle name, Chase, is in honor of him. He is important later in the story of my father's childhood.

Chase's father, Frank Doster (1847-1933), was a respected lawyer and politician. He served as Chief Justice of the Supreme Court of Kansas from 1897 to 1903, and had an unsuccessful campaign for the US Senate in 1914. He grew up in Indiana and Illinois, and served in the Union Army at the age of 14, joining a militia (Co. G. 105 Ind. State Legion), to drive Morgan's Raiders out of Indiana. He used his father's name to enlist because he was underage. After his duty ended, he returned home to work on the family farm. It was shorthanded since his two older brothers had enlisted in the Union Army. By 1864 both of his brothers had died in the Civil War. Even though he was the last surviving child, young Frank decided to enlist on January 30, 1864, at Delphi, Indiana. He enlisted as a private in Company M of the Eleventh Indiana Cavalry. He was only 17 at the time and lied about his age like before and used his father's name so he would not get rejected. After the Civil War ended, he finished up his second tour of duty by guarding the cattle drives from Indians and rustlers on the Santa Fe Trail. He never saw an Indian, but fell in love with the frontier territories, particularly the Kansas territory.

After his second tour of duty ended he studied at Indiana University Law school. He married and started his family, then decided to practice law in Marion, Kansas, which at the time, was a frontier town and did not have any lawyers. He lived in a tent at first, and after building a house, he sent for his young family including his mother, to join him; his father had passed away shortly after he left home. Frank was a populist at first, then a republican, and held some state offices. He was a defender of farmers' rights from landowners, including the railways and cattlemen, when they would divide the farmers' fields by placing rail lines through the farms and destroy the crops by driving cattle over their fields. He stated, "The rights of the user are paramount to the rights of the owner.". He even helped pass laws for farmers to legally use the new invention of barbed wire to guard their fields from the stampeding cattle. He moved to Topeka after being appointed to the Supreme Court of Kansas and was appointed Chief Justice. After retiring from the Supreme Court he continued to practice law in Topeka, ran for the US Senate in 1914, and later returned to his law practice until he suffered a stroke at age 84 and passed away.

Frank Doster's wife, Caroline Doster (born Riddle) (1847-1947), Dorothy's grandmother, was a talented artist who lived to be 100. She had many stories of her adventures in Marion including befriending Indians and inviting them into their home. People asked if she could trust them with the family's silver and she replied that they had no use for it. "If they were to steal anything, they would take a blanket which was more valuable than gold and silver to them."

Dorothy's aunts and uncles on the Doster side of the family were also successful. Frank and Caroline Doster had seven children, two of whom died as infants. Chase's oldest sister Lenore Cooke (born Doster) (1871-1919), like her mother, was a talented artist. Lenore studied in New York City with the famous portrait artist, William Merritt Chase. Chase often used his students as models. One of his paintings "*Girl in a Japanese Costume",* closely resembles Lenore but the subject of the painting is not credited. I have a theory that Frank and Caroline Doster knew Chase in Indiana where they both lived at the time, and named their first son, Chase, after William Merritt Chase. I can't imagine parents at that time sending their young daughter to New York to study art without knowing the person she would be studying with. After Lenore graduated, Chase hired her to teach watercolor painting at his school, then called the Chase School of Art. In 1899 she was married in New York to a young law student, Henry L. Cooke. They moved back to his hometown of Chattanooga, Tennessee where he practiced law and she continued as an artist. In 1905, after six years of marriage, her husband passed away. After Henry's death, William Merritt Chase invited her again to teach watercolor painting in his school in New York. After two years of teaching, she left the school, about the same time as Chase left, because of disagreements with the other directors of the school who wanted to emphasize the modern art movement. Chase was a traditionalist and rejected the Impressionist and Modernist movements as did Lenore. He is mostly known for his portraits and dark, brooding colors. The name of the school was changed to the New York School of Art and years later, the Parsons School of Design. Chase continued painting and teaching around New York and California. He died in 1916. Lenore taught art at Kansas City High School after leaving New York. A few years later she developed a respiratory illness, probably TB, left Kansas, and relocated with her father to

Pasadena, California because it was believed the dry weather there would help with her illness. She passed away in 1919 from the disease, possibly from the 1919 Spanish flu epidemic. I have one of her paintings, as do my cousins and a family friend has another. I am currently trying to locate more of her art.

I have another theory about the name Chase. The famous Chief Justice of the Supreme Court, Salmon P. Chase, was known primarily for presiding over the impeachment of President Andrew Johnson. He was Chief Justice from 1864 to 1873, and Frank must have studied his decisions while attending law school. Frank could have named his first son Chase because of him.

Chase's younger brother, Captain Wade Doster (1880-1920), could be labeled the black sheep of the family. He was a surgeon in the Army and had two daughters, Lenore and Caroline, with his wife, Helena B. Wilson, who died at a young age. I am named after Lenore's husband, Peter Maroney, who was close to my parents and Dorothy. Her sister, Caroline, married lawyer Robert T. Price who later was appointed Chief Justice of the Supreme Court of Kansas, following in the footsteps of his wife's grandfather, Frank Doster. My parents were fond of them and they were friends of our family. Because they were orphaned very young, the two girls were raised by their grandparents, Frank and Caroline Doster. My grandmother, Dorothy, was about the same age as the girls and often visited them at the Doster home in Topeka, Kansas. I have contacted Helena's family members and found out Wade's marriage was troubled, and he probably was abusing her and killed her. Wade entered another relationship with Maud Musgrove after his first wife died. They had a difficult relationship and started quarreling when she suspected he was cheating on her. According to court records, she shot and killed him, then shot herself, but it was unclear whether or not Wade may had shot her first. She survived and went on trial for his murder, but the judge was lenient after learning she was defended in court by Wade's father, Frank Doster. I think Frank knew about how his son was and knew that she most likely shot him in self-defense.

Chase's youngest brother, John Doster (1885-1958), was a civil engineer and never married. He stayed in Topeka and worked with his father after contracting a tropical fever while serving in the Army in Mexico.

Chase's youngest sister, Irma Doster, was a talented musician. She studied violin at the National Conservatory of Music in New York, Northwestern University, and Columbia University. She had many performances in New York and around the world. She married twice and settled in Chicago with her husband, Charles S. Carpenter, and started a music school called "The Doster School of Musical Expression". She was also a composer and author. In 1914 her father, Frank Doster, ran for the Kansas US Senate seat. Irma and her sister-in-law Florence Doster (born Gumaer), the wife of Chase Doster, campaigned with Frank, performing at his rallies. Unfortunately, he lost the primary election, and fellow Topeka resident and lawyer, Charles Curtis, won the election, served in the Senate, and later became Vice President to Herbert Hoover. He is important later in this story.

Dorothy's mother, Florence Doster (born Gumaer) (1884-1959) came from a well-to-do Denver family. She was a talented vocalist and was studying opera in Germany and France, but had to return home when Germany went to war (the Second Boer War). She often performed in public and was a featured soprano soloist with the Denver Symphony Orchestra. After she returned from her studies abroad, Florence married Chase Doster. Her parents divorced and her father remarried and had two children. Florence's half-brother and half-sister were also musicians. Her Gumaer family roots go back to eastern New York state and Connecticut. The Gumaer family were Huguenots who escaped from France because of religious persecution. They settled in Orange County, New York where many of my Gumaer cousins still live.

Florence's only child, Dorothy Doster, had a privileged upbringing. She attended one of the finest private schools in Denver (the Kent School for Girls). Her father, Chase Doster, was stationed in many places across the US and the world but his family remained in Denver. Her father retired from the military and returned to the Gumaer family residence on Pennsylvania Avenue in Denver (now Pennsylvania Street).

Their home was a large Victorian style house with many rooms. Florence's widowed aunt, Laura Hill (born Nichols), also lived with them. It was actually Laura's house which she had built after her husband passed away in 1887. More about her later.

Sarah Gumaer (born Nichols), Florence's divorced mother, and later another sister, Charlotte (Lottie) Nichols (1844-1933), all lived in the Pennsylvania Avenue house. There were two other Nichols sisters, Augusta (Gussie) Nichols who died while in childbirth shortly after her husband died, and Christine Gumaer (born Nichols) (1853-1945), who married Henry Gumaer who I believe is a relative of Sara's husband, J.D. Gumaer (probably his brother or cousin). They also had a brother, Edward Taylor Nichols Jr. The children were all born in Ohio, but relocated to Greeley, Colorado after their father experiencing legal problems in Ohio.

Members of the Nichols family were internationally famous. Their father, Edward Taylor Nichols (1816-1899), was the son of Laura Nichols (born Taylor), sister of P.T.'s Barnum's mother, Irena Barnum (born Taylor). Laura is the aunt of P.T. Barnum. My great-great-great grandfather, Edward Taylor Nichols, is a first cousin of P.T. Barnum.

Edward and P.T. Barnum grew up together in Connecticut. They were close in age, Barnum being six years older. As Barnum became wealthy and famous, he involved Edward in his business dealings. As Barnum's wealth increased he became increasingly paranoid that people were trying to cheat him. Barnum was a master of the "humbug" which basically means that he promoted deceptions and fake objects to gain money. I think he thought people were trying to fool him like he fooled many people who paid to see his fake exhibits.

Barnum thought his cousin Edward was trying to cheat him while he was taking care of business deals in Ohio for Barnum. In the 1850s Edward had been signing Barnum's name to mortgage documents and even sold Barnum autographs that Edward himself had signed. Barnum was outraged when he found out, and had Edward arrested for fraud. As a result, Edward spent a short time in jail. To plead his case, Edward produced documents from Barnum stating that he gave Edward permission to sign documents for him. Barnum's failed business dealings eventually led him into bankruptcy. Edward stayed in Ohio for a number of years growing his family, but his legal troubles lasted for years. Barnum did not hate his cousin and even gave him money to tide him over after he was released from jail. In the late 1860s Edward moved to Colorado with his family with the help of Barnum. Edward was given land in the Territory of Colorado (1861-1876) by grant deed from the US government. The land was later included in the Union Colony of Colorado that was being formed by New York Post writer Nathan Meeker.

Barnum had given up drinking and along with his friend Horace Greeley, the editor of the New York Post, backed the founding of Meeker's Union Colony, with money and land purchases, which was organized by Meeker. The colony was later named after its main benefactor Horace Greeley. Edward T. Nichols joined the colony which was founded on principles of Christianity and temperance (no drinking of alcohol allowed). Edward owned a grocery store located on Barnum's property, and he and his family lived on the land that he had received from the grant. Edward helped Barnum develop one of his properties in the colony by supervising the building of a hotel. Edward's family was interested in the arts and they produced plays that were performed in the upstairs of his grocery store before a theater was built some years later by Barnum. Later Barnum bought the Nichols property and had the theater constructed, he, of course, named it the Barnum Theater. The Nichols family then moved to Denver after the sale of their land to Barnum.

P.T. Barnum visited his cousin's family a number of times for family events and business dealings. His daughter, Helen Buchtel (born Barnum) (1840-1915), also lived in Denver after relocating there with her new husband, Dr. William Buchtel (1845-1912), who had contracted tuberculosis. The Buchtel name is well represented in Colorado. William's brother, Henry, was involved in Colorado politics and was elected the 17th governor of Colorado in 1907.

The family was also instrumental in the territory becoming a state.

Barnum had also invested in real estate in Denver in an area later named Villa Park, and had a house built for his daughter, Helen, and her husband. He also built a treatment center for tuberculosis which later became a hotel. The part of Villa Park that Barnum bought was then incorporated and named Barnum. Edward T. Nichols was one of the managers of Villa Park. Barnum later sold it to his daughter, Helen, for one dollar, which later made her one of the richest women in Colorado. The neighborhood still exists and is part of the city of Denver, and an elephant statue was erected in a local park as a nod to its founder. Later the area became famous for the discovery of dinosaur fossils.

P.T. Barnum only visited Colorado five times but on his last visit in 1890, a year before his death, he attended a party in his honor at the home of his daughter, Helen, which was attended by the Nichols family, as well as all the Denver socialites. It is most likely that my great-grandmother, Florence Gumaer, attended this party. She would have been about six years old at the time, and was living in Denver with her mother and the rest of the Nichols family, including Edward Sr., Edward Jr., and Laura Nichols Hill, in Denver. The new house on Pennsylvania Street was not completed yet. Barnum passed away the next year in 1891.

Barnum was a revered American icon and a celebrity. Words we still use today like "jumbo" are attributed to Barnum. Jumbo was the name of an African elephant that P.T. saw while visiting the London Zoo. He bought Jumbo from the zoo and shipped him to New York to be displayed in his arena called the "Great Roman Hippodrome". He named it that because he had it built to display a live hippopotamus, horse races, and other wonders of the animal kingdom. Later he sold the arena to the city and the name was changed to "Madison Square Garden". He also took Jumbo on tour with his circus. The Elephant died after being struck by a train. The word Jumbo comes from a Swahili word, "jambo", which means "hello", or "jumbe" meaning "chief".

Florence's mother, Sarah J. Gumaer (born Nichols) (1854-1945), has roots going back to colonial Connecticut. The Barnum family also was from Connecticut. Florence's grandmother, Sarah's mother, Sarah L. Nichols (born Bidwell) (1821-1883), the wife of P.T. Barnum's cousin Edward T. Nichols, is the granddaughter of General Benjamin Bidwell (1744-1831), who reinforced General Washington on the Hudson in 1777. Most of the Bidwell family came from England and settled in Connecticut and Massachusetts in the great Puritan migration in the early 1600s.

The wealth of Dorothy's family was mostly from one source, Dorothy's great aunt, Laura Hill (born Nichols) (1849-1927), daughter of Edward T. Nichols. Her husband, Wilbur H. Hill (1839-1887), made his fortune in the lumber business. Laura and Wilbur Hill did not have any children.

When he died in 1887 he left his estate to his wife, his young niece Florence Gumaer, and a brother and sister. In his will he left $200,000 to Laura (about $20 million in 2020 dollars adjusted for inflation), and $25,000 to his three-year-old niece, Florence (about $700,000 in 2020 dollars adjusted for inflation). After Wilbur died, Laura moved in with the Nichols family in Denver, and had the house on Pennsylvania Street completed a few years later.

By 1959 both Nichols' aunts and Florence had passed away. Most of the old Victorian houses on Pennsylvania Street were bought by developers and torn down to build apartment buildings. Dorothy Doster was an heiress to her aunt Laura's estate, and the only heir to her mother Florence's estate. She was an only child and inherited all her mother's wealth.

At an early age Dorothy displayed talent and an interest in photography. Some of her prints are in my family's possession, the best of which she took on visits to Mexico. She spoke French and Spanish fluently, as most girls of high society did at that time. She was tall and thin like her father, and very elegant. She was a teenager in the roaring 20s, a much more liberal time than the time of her parents. She was interested in the arts, knowledgeable in the modern painting masters, and literature, a true high society girl. After Dorothy graduated from Kent School for Girls, she was interested in a career as an artistic photographer even though she led a life of privilege and never had to worry about making a living. She never got to realize her dream.

In 1929, at age 19, a year after graduating from Kent, my grandmother's life changed drastically. She married French poet, Jean Tristan Hyacinthe Loyson, and after two years she was a divorced single mother. A short time after the divorce Jean Loyson passed away. My grandmother married a second time in 1932 to Giles Wetherill of the noted Philadelphia Wetherill family. That is why my last name is Wetherill, but it is complicated on how that came about. I will explain further in a later chapter.

The Wetherills were one of the richest families in Philadelphia and in the US. The Wetherill mansion on Rittenhouse Square is now the Philadelphia Art Alliance. Giles' grandfather willed it to the city in the 1920s. The family members were scions of the industrial revolution with inventions ranging from lead-free paint to the invention of a zinc ore smelter. South Bethlehem, Pennsylvania is where the Wetherill factories were located, and at that time the town was called Wetherill.

The Wetherill ancestors were Quakers who escaped when the King of England was jailing them after refusing to serve in the British military because of their religious beliefs, such as "Though shalt not kill".

Many Quakers who supported the Revolution were forced out of the Quaker religion because it does not even let them contribute or support any military action whatsoever.

Samuel Wetherill (1736-1816), Giles' 4x great-grandfather, and other Quakers, defended Philadelphia during the Revolution. In 1781 they started their own branch of the Quaker religion called the Free Quakers, and were acknowledged by the founding fathers for their support. Samuel Wetherill was one of the few makers of cloth in the colonies (England did not like this, preferring all the colonial cotton to be sent to England for manufacturing, and only English ships were allowed to import cloth to the colonies). This rule and the Revolution created shortages of cloth which caused General Washington to have problems securing materials for his Army's uniforms. Samuel donated the cloth for the uniforms of Washington's Army. Betsy Ross was also a Free Quaker and close friend of Samuel and his family. She later gave him the star pattern for the first US flag. The star was handed down from generation to generation. Later, after the family mansion was built, the star pattern was kept in the mansion's safe. After the mansion was donated to the city, the star was moved to the Free Quaker museum church where it is on display today. There are more connections to the rest of the family which I will get to later in this book.

CHAPTER 2

My Father's Father's Family

My father's father, Jean Tristan Hyacinthe Loyson (1902-1931), was born in Geneva, Switzerland. He was a French citizen born to celebrated French playwright Paul Hyacinthe Loyson (1873-1921), and his US born wife Laura Jayne Loyson (born Bucknell) (1871-1958). The family lived and traveled throughout Europe. Paul Loyson's plays were performed around the world and still are today. Paul was also multilingual and served as a translator for the leaders of France, notably, for the diplomatic effort to prevent the start of WWI. Young Jean lived in Germany, France, Italy, and Switzerland, but the family home was in Paris, France. To know more about my grandfather, Jean, it is important to know about his family.

Jean's paternal grandparents were internationally known religious figures who started their own church in Paris. They also had a home in Geneva, where Jean and his father, Paul, were born. Jean's paternal Grandfather, Charles Jean Marie Augustin Loyson (1827-1912), better known by his liturgical name, Père Hyacinthe Loyson, was a Catholic Priest and the head of the Discalced, (barefoot), Carmelite Monks of Paris. He left the clergy and his order after questioning the Ecumenical Council's 1869 decision that proclaimed the Pope as infallible.

Jean's paternal grandmother, Emilie Jane Meriman Loyson (born Butterfield) (1833-1909), met Père Hyacinthe after her decision to leave the 1st Baptist Church of Brooklyn, New York and convert to Catholicism while visiting Europe. He was assigned to teach and guide her in her conversion, and they became close friends during the process. She was born in western New York, but her family relocated to the frontier town of Melmore, Ohio when she was a young child. Life was difficult for the family and there were many losses. Her youngest brother died in infancy and her father, Amory Butterfield (1792-1836), died in an accident while building the First Methodist Church of Melmore. Most of the men in her father's family were preachers, including her father.

Despite the difficulties of frontier life, she had an excellent education. Her mother, Mary (Polly) Butterfield (born Lamb) (1793-1869), had been the main influence in her life, as her father had passed away when she was only 3. Mary descended from a long line of Protestant preachers from western New York and Boston, one of whom, her grandfather, Pastor David Lamb (1745-1820), was purported to have baptized Joseph Smith, the founder of the Mormon Church. One of Mary's brothers, Abel Lamb, became a friend of Joseph Smith and joined the movement. When Smith was murdered, Abel continued on to Salt Lake City with many of the other followers, and is considered one of the founders of the Mormon Church.

In her younger years, Emilie was hired as a public school teacher in her hometown, and after her marriage to Edwin Ruthven Meriman, she became a published writer. She had two children with Edwin; Ralph Meriman (1854-1938), and Mary Meriman (1858-1863). Mary died in childhood and Ralph became an architect. Ralph is important and controversial, which I will explain later in this chapter. Emilie's writings include many articles in multiple newspapers, journals, books, and the translation of books from French to English. She was well-educated and wrote mostly about religion. I have transcribed and published her handwritten autobiography which she never able to do because of failing health; Autobiography Volume 1: THE EVOLUTION OF THE SOUL FROM THE GREAT AMERICAN FOREST TO THE VATICAN COUNCIL, by MADAME HYACINTHE LOYSON, Peter Chase Wetherill, editor.

Jean Hyacinthe's family was wealthy. Paul Hyacinthe Loyson, his father, was an internationally renowned playwright, and Jean's mother, Laura Jayne Loyson (born Bucknell) (1871-1958), was an American born double heiress. Her paternal grandfather, William Robert Bucknell Jr. (1811-1890), was the namesake and primary benefactor of Bucknell University. He made his fortune investing in railways, tramways, gas companies and the stock market. At his death in 1890, he was one of the richest men in Philadelphia, worth $7,000,000, equivalent to almost $200,000,000 in 2020 dollars. He was a trustee of the First Baptist Church of Philadelphia as well as primary benefactor of Bucknell University (at the time named the University of Lewisburg). After his death the name was changed in honor of Bucknell. One of his stipulations for his donations to the University was that it would allow women to attend. This was unprecedented at the time and as a result, many other universities followed suit.

Laura's maternal grandfather, Dr. David Jayne (1799-1866), was the first doctor to patent his own medicines. He became very wealthy from his idea, and invested heavily in Philadelphia real estate which increased his wealth even more. He needed a building in Philadelphia to manufacture his medicines and for his business offices, but land was expensive, so he had a multi-storied building built on a narrow lot. He even had a steam-driven lift installed, before elevators were invented, to access the upper floors. His building is considered one of the first skyscrapers in the US. It later burned to the ground some years after his death. His medicine business continued and was run by his business partners and family members. Dr. Jayne's Root Beer was on the market well into the 20th century. He was also active in the First Baptist Church of Philadelphia. At his death he was worth more than $3,000,000, (about $50,000,000 in 2020 dollars), but income from his business continued well into the 20th century. Laura inherited much wealth from the Bucknell and Jayne estates, in addition to her husband Paul's estate. Her mother (also named Laura) is the daughter of David Jayne. She is also important and controversial, which I will explain later in this chapter.

All of the wealth from the family passed down to Jean's mother, Laura Jayne Loyson (born Bucknell) after the death of her husband Paul in 1921. Laura had a sister, Berthe Jayne Chapman (born Bucknell) (1870-1938), who also inherited a share of the Bucknell and Jayne fortunes. Laura became the matriarch of the family. Jean had two sisters, Marthe, and Emilie Pauline, and a brother, Charles, who died in infancy.

Jean's parents, Paul and Laura, met as children in Geneva. They were distant cousins through Paul's mother Emilie Jane Loyson. When Paul was a student he was tutored in English by Laura's mother, Laura Bucknell (born Jayne) (1848-?). Laura Bucknell's two daughters, Laura and Berthe, were both playmates of Paul. Paul later married Laura, and Berthe married American, Samuel Hudson Chapman (1857-1931), an internationally known numismatist, and they lived in Philadelphia after marriage. Laura Bucknell left the US for Geneva after her husband, William Rufus Babcock Bucknell (1847-1885), passed away, and lived close to her sister, Hannah Hopkins (born Jayne) (1845-1900), and her husband, William Alonzo Hopkins (1841-1928), who was a newspaper publisher, and were close friends with the Loysons. William's mother was Laura Hopkins (born Butterfield) and a first cousin to Emilie. Emilie wrote articles for his newspaper. The Hopkins family plays an important role later in this story.

The Loyson, Hopkins, and Bucknell families all lived in the same neighborhood in Geneva and probably on the same street. Emilie Loyson's son Ralph Meriman lived there until he started his studies in architecture in the US. After graduating he worked as an architect in Washington, D.C. and married Kate C. Wheatly. They had a son named Paul Hyacinthe (probably named after Ralph's half-brother Paul Hyacinthe Loyson). A few years later they divorced and Ralph returned to Europe and began a romantic relationship which led to a second marriage. This was controversial for his family. On December 19, 1897, he married Laura Bucknell (born Jayne), the neighbor and tutor of his half-brother Paul! Laura was only six years older than Ralph. This must have ruffled some feathers in the family. In 1896 Paul had married Laura Bucknell's daughter Laura. That made a strange family relationship. Laura Loyson (born Bucknell) became Ralphs' stepdaughter and sister-in-law! Ralph was Pauls' half-brother and stepfather. My grandfather Jean Loysons' maternal grandmother, Laura Bucknell (born Jayne) was his grandmother and his aunt. This makes my head spin!

Père Hyacinthe was preaching at local churches in Geneva before he and Emilie returned to Paris to start his own church. They had many fundraising trips abroad including tours in the US. Paul often traveled with them. One of the trips they took was to North Africa and the Middle East. The object of this tour was to try to arrange a meeting of the religious leaders of the Christian, Muslim, and Jewish faiths so they could broker a peace agreement between their religions. The leaders never could agree to meet, and the followers of these faiths continue killing each other to this day. Emilie wrote a book about their journey which is still on sale today: "To Jerusalem through the Lands of Islam: Among Jews, Christians, and Moslems" (1905) by Emilie Jane Butterfield Meriman Loyson."

Paul's mother away in 1909 and his father in1912, and Paul continued in the pacifist movement, the same as his parents, and believed that another war in Europe would not solve any of the political conflicts of that time. He was involved as a translator to French politicians and diplomats who were sent on international missions to try to quell the hostilities that were brewing. They failed, and "The Great War to end all wars" started. They were correct in their beliefs. Young Jean served in the French military after the war, as required by French Law. One of the only photos I have of him is in his uniform. Jean's father, Paul, passed away in 1921. Jean had made friends throughout Europe during the family's travels. While living in Rome he became best friends with young Italian poet, Lauro de Bosis, who later became an anti-fascist protester who died after distributing leaflets over Rome from a small airplane. He is important in a later chapter of this book.

CHAPTER 3

How My Grandparents Met

One of the greatest mysteries of all my research into the "French side" of my family; how Dorothy Doster met Jean Loyson. I have tried to trace both of their paths in the years before their marriage in August of 1929. My grandmother never talked about this part of her past. I have found more clues about my grandfather's travels due to four of his books of poetry. One of them has poems mentioning North America, and details about his best friend, Lauro de Bosis. Other clues have emerged from family letters uncovered by my cousin Carl Eschweiler.

My grandmother, Dorothy Doster, traveled around the US for visits to her father, relatives, and vacations. Her mother, Florence Doster (born Gumaer), was born in Saginaw, Michigan. Florence's father, J.D. Gumaer, was a traveling farm equipment salesman from southeastern New York state. He and his sales territory moved westward with the population, finally settling in Denver, Colorado, where he divorced his wife Sarah J. Gumaer (born Nichols) and remarried.

After Dorothy graduated from Kent in 1928, she was accepted to study at the Paris branch of the School of Applied and Fine Arts. She turned 18 that summer and travelled to Paris accompanied by her parents who arranged for her to stay with a French family who also hosted another American student, Elizabeth Chase, the daughter of Charles A. Chase. Dorothy's parents then continued traveling after she had settled into her new life in Paris. I discovered this from a Denver Post announcement from December, 1928. I don't have proof, but it would seem logical that she met Jean Loyson in Paris.

It is a bit easier to trace Jean Hyacinthe's travels. He has many links to the US through family and friends. His mother and both grandmothers were both from the US. His mother, Laura Jayne Loyson (born Bucknell) was probably born in Brooklyn, New York, where her parents were living at the time, although they were both originally from Philadelphia, Pennsylvania. Her father, William Babcock Bucknell, was the son of William Bucknell Jr. and his first wife, Harriet M. Bucknell (born Ashton), as mentioned earlier. The senior Bucknell was married three times. He married for the last time at 60 to 19-year-old Emma Eliza Ward (1853-1927), the daughter of Baptist missionaries, in India, who was born at a mission in India which William Bucknell helped to finance.

Bucknell's main residence was in Philadelphia but he owned many properties, and shortly after his death his widow built Pine Point Lodge on Upper Saranac Lake, New York, as a summer vacation house. Emma sold most of his properties and also bought a winter home in Clearwater, Florida. She had four children and didn't remarry. I know much about her from a biography centering around her voyage on the ill-fated Titanic, titled "Emma Eliza Bucknell: Titanic Survivor" by D. Flodin Soderman. After her death, the lodge passed to her children and they spent many summers there well into the 20th century. I have photos of my father and his brother at that lodge when they were boys. The Titanic is involved in one of my theories on how they met.

I can place my grandfather in this area in the summer of 1928 through his poetry. Two poems of that year are dated between June and July at Lake Placid and one at Montreal. Lake Placid is one of the Finger Lakes next to Saranac Lake. I am sure he must have stayed at the lodge, most likely with other family members, one of which plays an important part of the story later. Also mentioned in family letters to the Hopkins family was his desire to visit them in Wisconsin where the Hopkins family was living. He was very fond of this family. One of his poems clearly shows he is in love but he doesn't say whom:

Le ciel si clair, si pur...

Le ciel si clair, si pur, le soleil dans les feuilles,
    Le grand lac bleu qui rêve
Et sur ses bords, au loin, la brise qui se lève,
    L'odeur du chèvrefeuille,

Le clapotis de l'eau sur les marches de pierre
    Et l'ombre d'un oiseau
Qui glisse, fugitive, au miroir de l'eau,

Le vol des éphémères

Qui dansent au soleil leur ronde vive et brève,
    -Ah ! qu'importe cela,
Qu'importe l'horizon, les pays où les rêves
    Puisque tu n'es pas là !

Lake Placid, 25 Juin 1928

Rough translation:

The sky so clear, so pure ...

The sky so clear, so pure, the sun in the leaves,
    The big blue lake that dreams
And on its edges, in the distance, the breeze that rises,
    The smell of honeysuckle,

The rippling water on the stone steps
    And the shadow of a bird
Who slips, fugitive, to the mirror of the water,
    The flight of ephemera

Who dance in the sun their lively and brief round,
   -Ah! what does it matter?
Whatever the horizon, the countries were dreams
   Since you're not here!

Lake Placid, June 25, 1928

   This poem could be about Dorothy or another love. She would have turned 18 that summer and a year after this poem she was pregnant with my father! A poem that my grandfather wrote in December seems to be about someone he is in love with but absent from his home in Paris. The poems in the years before this are about lost love, missing someone, or someone that he loved that has died. I conclude that the December poem, which is the last that I've found, must be about Dorothy, and that a few months after this, my father was conceived.

   Another reason that Jean would have traveled to the US would be to visit his best friend Lauro de Bosis. Lauro's girlfriend at the time was stage actress and comedian Ruth Draper. It was the beginning of their love affair that lasted three years until his death. In the fall of 1928 Lauro traveled to the US to accept a position with the Italy-American Society which is in Philadelphia. I don't know if Jean was there or when he traveled back to France. I know from passenger lists that Jean arrived in New York on May 28, 1928, but in 2020 Ancestry.com only lists arrivals to the US so

I don't know when he left to go back to France. There are some clues in his poetry from 1928. He wrote a poem in Montreal on July 17, a poem about an ocean liner on July 16, two poems about lake Placid on June 25 and August 14. On January 19 he wrote a lullaby about an infant boy with no location given, but it must be in France, since he arrived in the US on May 28. As mentioned before, on December 28 he wrote a poem about Paris at dusk. It seems to be about missing a romantic partner. It is possible that Jean, Dorothy, and her parents sailed to Paris on the same ocean liner and met there at the end of the summer.

The meeting on the liner seems plausible, and they both arrived in Paris after the summer. There is a mention in one of his books of poems from 1930 of an upcoming book of poems that was to be released in 1931, but I have not found evidence that the book was ever published. If so, it probably would have poems about my grandmother and my father.

I may never discover how my grandparents met, but I have one more theory, which came to my mind while researching the Titanic! It might seem farfetched today, but at the time of my grandparents' marriage, the members of high society, the extremely wealthy, fell into similar social circles that time were mostly bound to geographical areas, primarily big American cities, such as New York, Chicago, Philadelphia, and some of the newer cities like Denver. The very wealthy could afford international leisure travel, something that is easy and inexpensive for most people today.

In the past, the only way to cross any ocean was by ship. The first-class passengers on these ocean liners were separated from the steerage class, and knew each other from their social circles. They would dine and entertain together and sometimes plan trips together. Both my Denver and Philadelphia families would travel in first-class.

One member of my family who would travel frequently as a first-class passenger on these luxurious liners was Emma Eliza Bucknell (born Ward). She was the third wife of William Bucknell. William Bucknell died in 1890 and his widow, Emma, immediately became very wealthy. William had married her, shortly after his second wife died, when he was sixty years old and she was only nineteen, as mentioned before. This was a bit scandalous at the time but not so unusual. They had four children: Margaret, Howard, Edith, and Trudy. Edith married Samuel Wetherill and had four children, one of which was Giles, mentioned earlier as the second husband of my grandmother, Dorothy. Samuel Wetherill, his children, and grandchildren often spent summers at the lodge on Saranac Lake.

The Bucknells' daughter, Margaret, had a stormy first marriage which ended in divorce. While on a trip to Rome she met and fell in love with Count Daniel Pecorini, a member of the Italian royal family. After they married in 1906, they lived in Rome. Margaret was a talented artist and Daniel was a writer, poet and also an art collector. After their marriage in 1906, Emma would visit her in Rome on a yearly basis. During these voyages she met many members of society types. She had many things in common with one of these; both had come from poor families and married into wealth and both of them had daughters that were artists. Her name was Margaret Brown from Denver, Colorado. If that name seems familiar, the nickname that was given to her later in life was; "the Unsinkable Molly Brown"!

Upon reading biographies of Margaret Brown I learned that after her husband discovered gold in the mines of Colorado, they moved to Denver and bought a large house on Pennsylvania Avenue in the early 1890s. As mentioned in Chapter One of this book, The Nichols, Hill, and Gumaer families also built a house on Pennsylvania Avenue just down the street from the Brown home. This street was lined with homes of Denver's rich and famous. Margaret used her wealth to educate herself and travel the world. In 1902 she embarked on a world tour with her husband,. Margaret wrote articles for the Denver Post about their travels. A few years later she separated from her husband. Margaret continued to travel but because of separating from her husband she traveled alone. During these travels she became friends with Emma Bucknell and they frequently traveled and even toured Paris with their daughters. Margaret had a daughter that was studying art at the Sorbonne in

Paris and Emma would often visit the Louvre and shop for art with her daughter, Margaret.

In 1912 Margaret Brown and Emma Bucknell sailed to Europe but had not planned to return on the same ship. Emma's son, Howard was receiving a degree in Medicine so she was going to arrive early and leave in time for the graduation. Margaret was traveling with her daughter Helen to Paris, and Emma was visiting her daughter in Rome. They both ended up changing their return travel plans after Margaret's grandson was taken ill in Denver, and Emma wanted to make sure that she made it home in time for her son's graduation. They both changed their plans and booked passage on a new ship, the Titanic!

They both boarded the ship in Cherbourg, France but didn't know they were both traveling together until Emma saw Margaret getting ready to board the tender to the Titanic, which was moored offshore because the Titanic, was too big for the dock. Of course they spotted each other and were delighted to travel together again. Emma then told Margaret that she had forebodings about the trip, but Margaret said that she should not worry since the Titanic was unsinkable! When they both arrived in the US after surviving the Titanic sinking, they formed a charity together to help the survivors and families of the lost souls of the Titanic.

Here is my conjecture as to how Jean Loyson and Dorothy Doster might have met. Margaret Brown was also interested in acting and participated in the theater scene in Paris. Jean Loyson's father, Paul, was a famous playwright. Emma also must have visited her family in Paris, William Bucknell's grandchildren, Laura Jayne Loyson (born Bucknell) and her family. They probably all knew each other. And in Denver, the Nichols, Gumaer, and Hill families most likely knew their neighbors down the street, the Browns. It is possible that the young Dorothy Doster might have been introduced to the Loyson

s and Bucknells through Margaret Brown. Both Margaret and Dorothy were living in Paris after 1928. It is possible that the idea of Dorothy studying art in Paris was suggested to Dorothy and her parents by Margaret, since her own daughter had studied there. When Dorothy arrived in Paris she could have been introduced to the Loyson family by Margaret. Of course this is a theory, and Dorothy probably fell in love with her professor Jean Loyson at the school of arts at the Sorbonne where he and many of the Loysons had lectured and taught, or perhaps she met him on her voyage to Paris. I think the latter is more likely but the Margaret Brown Titanic connection is more entertaining!

CHAPTER 4

Marriage, Divorce, and the Birth of My Father

On August 28, 1929, my grandparents, Jean Hyacinthe Tristan Loyson and Dorothy Doster, were wed in Chelsea, Great Britain. I know Dorothy's mother, Florence Doster, was at the wedding, because she left Chelsea and arrived in New York on September 9, as recorded in a New York Passenger list. After the wedding the newlyweds returned to Paris and started their honeymoon travels along the coast of France. They were searching out properties along the French Riviera to buy, which they later did. Five months later, the newlyweds were in Paris for the birth of my father! Dorothy's mother also traveled to Paris for the birth. I have his French birth certificate showing the place of birth, as well as an announcement in the Denver Post. In the US they call this a shotgun marriage, so Jean and Dorothy must have been romantically involved before May of 1929, which is nine months before my father was born.

My father did not know the date of his parents' marriage until the 1960s when we were visiting my grandmother in Denver. He was looking for some legal papers and happened to find the wedding certificate and did the math. He did not take this too seriously and often, jokingly, referred to himself as a bastard child of a French poet. Of course this is inaccurate since they were married when he was born, but he was conceived before they were married. Since pregnancy tests were not available in drug stores like today, Dorothy probably did not realize that she was pregnant for a few months after conception, probably sometime in the summer of 1929, maybe three months later, around July or August. The discovery of her pregnancy would have led to their quick marriage in England.

My father was born Loys Aurilien Loyson in Paris, France on January 26, 1930. Over the next year or so, his parents relocated to southern France in Antibes at the villa that they had bought to live in as a married couple. On February 27, 1931, Dorothy took Loys to the US embassy in Nice to get a visa so my father could travel to and enter the US. He could not be ifledncluded on Dorothy's US passport since he was a French citizen and, she stated, he was too young to get a French passport. The Vice-Consul wrote a letter explaining the problem and issued a visa for 12 months. She then traveled to Italy and boarded an Italian ship that headed to Cherbourg, France, and then crossed the Atlantic on another ship, arriving in New York on March 30, 1931. My father was admitted by the Immigration Inspector for a visit to the US for six months.

Dorothy then returned to her parents' house in Denver, Colorado. In August she traveled to Reno, Nevada to file for divorce, leaving Loys to be cared for by his grandparents, Florence and Chase. She was notified that Jean had filed for divorce in France and that the French court had given him the divorce and custody of my father. Jean then traveled to the US with the intention to take his son back to France, and arrived in New York on May 5, 1931. In August he was notified of the divorce proceedings in Reno, so he traveled there to appear at the divorce court to attempt to get full custody. He traveled to Reno with the help of his cousin, Giles P. Wetherill (grandson of William Bucknell), who at the same time, was seeking a divorce from his first wife. Jean is the great- grandson of William Bucknell. Jean might have been staying with him in Philadelphia, but he had many relatives in the area including the Jaynes and his aunt Berthe Chapman who also lived there.

A "Decree of Divorce" was granted to Dorothy "on the grounds the defendant's failure to provide the plaintiff with the common necessaries of life, and extreme cruelty." On September 1, 1931, custody of Loys was granted to Dorothy. Jean was ordered to pay $50 a month for child support, and he was allowed to visit at reasonable times and places. The French divorce was deemed invalid since Dorothy was a US citizen and not given the chance to testify in the French proceeding.

I am not sure of the spelling of my father's middle name. His French Birth certificate looks like Aurilian, the divorce papers Aurlian, and some other papers Aurelian. All of them are legitimate names. This will change, anyway, which I will explain in the next chapter.

After the divorce was finalized, Dorothy returned to Denver to be reunited with and raise Loys. Giles Price Wetherill, her new love interest, went with her, (they must have met in Reno!). They did not live with Dorothy's parents but lived in another house in Denver from 1931 to 1932. In 1932 they moved to Giles' apartment in Philadelphia's Rittenhouse Square, leaving Loys with her parents. Later Dorothy's parents officially adopted Loys.

In September, a short time after the divorce, Jean returned to Paris and became romantically involved with his cousin, Winifred Hopkins. She was the granddaughter of the sister of Jean's maternal grandmother, Laura Bucknell (born Jayne), Hannah Hopkins (born Jayne), mentioned earlier. Jean and Winifred were childhood friends. Shortly after returning to France he proposed marriage to her. I suspect they already had a relationship before he met Dorothy, but their relationship must have been frowned upon by the family, as they were first cousins.

Then there was a major loss in Jean's life. His longtime and best friend, Lauro de Bosis, had started the anti-fascist movement, Alleanza Nazionale, to protest Mussolini and Fascism. One main objective was to distribute anti-fascist newsletters across Italy. He left his position in the Italy-America society in December, 1930. Upon returning to Italy, he learned that two of his collaborators in the movement, as well as his mother, were arrested. His mother was released but the two collaborators were sentenced to 15 years in prison.

In the summer of 1931 in Corsica, Lauro started taking flying lessons and bought a small airplane for the purpose of delivering anti-fascist leaflets over Rome. His plans were discovered while he was in Corsica and he had to escape and go into hiding in France for fear that Mussolini would have him killed. He bought another plane in Germany and had it flown to Southern France. At this time Jean had returned to France and was probably there with him in Antibes. I suspect Jean helped him finance his anti-fascist activities. On October 14, Lauro took off from France, but before heading to Rome passed over Jean's villa while he was sick in bed. While dropping leaflets over Rome at low altitude he passed over where Mussolini was staying. Mussolini was furious and scrambled the Italian Air Force to stop him, but he flew out to sea before they could shoot him down. He did not make it back to France and probably ran out of fuel and crashed into the sea. Neither he nor his plane was never found.

The divorce, losing custody of Loys, and the death of his best friend must have devastated Jean. A month later, on November 14, 1931, Jean passed away. It was only two months after returning to France. The newspapers said he had died of a tropical illness (malaria) contracted while he served in the French Army in Morocco. I have doubts that this was the case, since he was healthy enough to travel back and forth to the US only a few months before. I thought that the only way to learn the cause of death would be to see his death certificate, but after inquiring, I found French death certificates do not list cause of death. The only way to learn his official cause of death would be to contact the hospital where he was treated or taken after dying, and see his medical records, but I have no idea what hospital it would be or even if the records would have survived WWII! I don't even know where he was when he died. A biography of Lauro's girlfriend, Ruth Draper, says that he was in Antibes a month before his death. All of his family members that were alive then, have passed away. Winnie's son Carl Eschweiler says his mother only knew of his death from the newspapers which said he died of a tropical disease at his mother's home in Paris.

CHAPTER 5

BREAKING THE LAW AND BECOMING A LEGAL RESIDENT OF THE US

With that background in place, we now reach my main reason for writing this book: How wealth and connections helped my father become a US citizen. During the divorce of his parents in Reno, my father, a French citizen, was living with his grandparents, Chase and Florence Doster, in Denver, Colorado. After the divorce, he was living with his mother and her fiancée, Giles Wetherill in Denver, On August 30, 1931, six months after leaving France, he overstayed his visa and became an undocumented immigrant, or as many would say, he broke the law and became an illegal immigrant. A few months later his father would pass away.

His grandparents were concerned about his legal status and started sending inquiries to the US government asking how to resolve the situation and make him a legal resident and US citizen. My great grandfather, Chase Doster, was a career Army man and retired as a Colonel. He knew who to contact. They officially adopted my father, but since he was a French citizen in the country illegally, the adoption did not give him the right to become a US citizen. French law did not recognize the adoption of a French minor by foreign parents outside of France. This was a big problem.

Chase then contacted the Vice President of the US, Hon. Charles Curtis. Curtis was from Topeka, Kansas and was a rival of Chase's father, Frank Doster, some years earlier. Curtis was of American Indian descent and was mostly shunned by President Hoover, even though he was an experienced politician and US senator. He knew what to do to get my father legalized. VP Curtis then consulted with the Assistant Secretary of Labor, Robe Carl White, and he wrote a letter back to the VP explaining the rights of my father. I have which was forwarded to Loys' grandparents, which. The second paragraph outlines his rights or lack of rights:

"The Commissioner of Naturalization, within whose province this matter comes, informs me that on September 22, 1922, a statute was enacted to the effect that a woman citizen of the United States should not cease to be a citizen by reason of marriage to an alien. The correspondences which accompanied your communication states that there was no renunciation of American citizenship by Mrs. Loyson. There was, therefore, no loss of citizenship by her reason of her marriage on August 28, 1929. There having been no loss of citizenship, there was no resumption on her part whereby Section 5 of the act of March 2, 1907, could be brought into operation to confer citizenship on her child. Section 1993 of the United States Revised Statutes, which relates to children born abroad of American fathers, does not purport to children born abroad of an American mother and an Alien father. It appears, therefore, that the child is an alien."

In 1932, probably after her wedding on March 5, Dorothy and Giles Wetherill moved to Giles' apartment in Philadelphia and left Dorothy's parents to care for Loys in Denver. After this, Dorothy had more legal problems concerning the settlement of Jean's estate. Dorothy's divorce lawyer from Reno traveled to France to help settle Jean's estate. The meeting with the justice of the peace was set, not by Dorothy's lawyer, but by Jean's Mother, for June 21, 1932, to inventory his belongings at his villa with the family counselor, which should have been Dorothy or her representative. My father was his only heir. The reason the justice gave the position to Jean's mother was that Dorothy lost that right because she had remarried and did not inform the justice. Dorothy did not inform her lawyer who was in France, either, or he could have corrected the problem. Jean's mother found out, and brought newspaper clippings to prove she had wed. This was news to her lawyer, who, although he tried to delay the meeting, was only to manage a few days. This caused my father to not have any rights to his father's estate.

Dorothy was not concerned with receiving money from Jean's estate. She was more concerned about some papers that were still at the villa. She was not poor. Her aunt, Charlotte (Lottie) E. Hill (born Nichols), who had no children, left her estate to Dorothy and two other relatives. At the time, the estate was worth $126,000, equivalent to almost $2.4 million in 2020 dollars. Her new husband, Giles Wetherill was also extremely wealthy as mentioned in Chapter 1 of this book.

Dorothy's parents wanted to make Loys a legal US citizen, but they did not know how to do this. They discovered a way about a year later, probably with the advice of the US government or their personal lawyer. In other words, my father could have been deported for not being a legal resident of the US! This is not a federal criminal offense but a civil offense controlled by immigration. If caught, my father would not be charged with a crime and sent to jail (since he was a minor), but could be judged by immigration court and sent back to his relatives in France. Dorothy and her parents wanted to prevent that from happening.

I don't know who advised them on how to "legalize" my father, but the plan worked. My father needed to leave the US and obtain a green card before returning, but if his grandparents took him to France to do this, his French family could have legally taken custody of him because of his father's French divorce proceedings. They must have ruled that out!

This is how they did it: On February 3, 1933 they traveled to the French Consulate in San Francisco and applied for a French passport issued in my father's name. After being approved for the passport on February 25, they traveled to

Juarez, Mexico and visited the US consulate there and applied for a green card for him to legally stay in the US. The rules for reentry into the US after overstaying a visa state that the person has to visit a US consulate outside of the US to receive permission to reenter. The only problem would be the US consul could have barred my father from entering the US for three to ten years since he overstayed his original visa. The US consul in Suarez granted the request and issued a green card for my father to enter and live in the US. He most likely approved his green card because his mother was a US citizen living in the US and he was a minor. Green cards are valid for ten years, so he could legally live in the US until his expired. When Loys' application was made, his grandparents changed his name to Frank Loyson-Doster for his green card. This name change helped keep my father out of trouble many years later. My father was then a legal resident of the US, but not a US citizen, even though his mother was.

A few years later Dorothy and Giles started their own family with the birth of their son, Samuel Price Wetherill on August 14, 1934. The Wetherills wanted to have the whole family together, so they requested that Dorothy's son, now named Frank, join them to live in Philadelphia. Florence and Chase were still concerned that Frank was not a US citizen, so Giles made legal inquiries about how to accomplish this. One way for Frank to gain his citizenship, was to be adopted by a US citizen. His grandparents' adoption did not count, since he was in the US as a French citizen on a visitor's visa. After consulting with his lawyer, Giles was assured that he could adopt Frank legally in Pennsylvania. Some states did not allow this at that time. All the legal papers were arranged and Frank was adopted by Dorothy and Giles Wetherill on May 6, 1936. Unfortunately, Chase had passed away in 1935 and did not get to see this happen. Finally, my father was a US citizen! He now had the name, Frank Loyson-Doster Wetherill. His parents didn't like this name so they changed the order to Frank Doster Loyson-Wetherill. This is not the last name change for my father, though…

CHAPTER 6

Life as a US Citizen

Finally, after six years, my father became a US citizen living in the city of our founding fathers, Philadelphia, with his mother, brother, and stepfather who adopted him as his own son. Giles was a big influence on my father since he was the only "father" that he knew.

Giles was from one of the wealthiest families of Philadelphia, and had a career even though he didn't have to work for a living. He was a partner in a Humus company and an engineer specializing in munitions. When WWII broke out he enlisted and was assigned to an engineering group for artillery and munitions. After the war he was hired to help rebuild the Italian government's armaments. This led to marital problems and Giles and Dorothy divorced in 1945.

Dorothy and the two boys returned to Denver to live with Dorothy's mother, their grandmother, Florence, in her old Victorian style house on Pennsylvania Street. All the aunts had died by this time and she was living alone with her little dog, so she welcomed her daughter and grandsons to live with her.

Frank and Sam were hellions and got into some trouble. Both boys were intelligent and got into things. My father loved model airplanes and ships, and his room was full of them, especially

WWII aircraft which he hung from the ceiling. The most destructive trouble they got into was when they were experimenting with explosives (remember their father Giles was a munitions engineer) and blew a hole in their grandmother's bathtub!

Young Frank was especially gifted in languages. He was so gifted that his mother took him out of school and hired a tutor for the remainder of his education. Recently I heard from a neighbor of his who reminisced that Frank was a geek, always carried a black satchel with him like a professor. He had a photographic memory and was an avid reader.

The Korean war broke out while Frank was studying Romance languages at the University of Colorado Boulder. After graduation, he enlisted in the Army, and in basic training was a crack shot. His stepfather, Giles Wetherill, was a munitions expert, an avid collector of firearms, and handmade custom knives, and taught Frank how to shoot at a young age. My father dreamed of becoming an Air Force pilot but he had bad eyesight, which excluded him. At 14 he took private flying lessons and got his pilot's license, even before he got his driver's license. After basic training he was assigned as a translator and sent to an Army base in France! He said that he didn't do much there and would translate for the nuns in a nearby mission. I think Giles pulled some strings to get him this post to keep him out of combat.

After his tour of duty ended, he stayed in France and continued his graduate level studies of Romance languages at the Sorbonne University in Paris. My father had a Dutch friend who was also studying languages there. She invited her best friend from The Hague, Hendrika Hilbers, who was studying French at the Lycée in The Hague, to visit her and introduced my father to her. It was love at first sight, and two weeks later my father asked for her hand in marriage. Hendrika Hilbers and Frank Doster Loyson-Wetherill were married in The Hague. They later returned to Boulder so my father could finish his master's degree in Romance Languages there.

My father visited his extended family while in France. Jean's younger sister Pauline had married surgeon Paul Chigot who was the son of famous artist Eugene Chigot. Paul had a key role in WWII running a surgical unit near front lines with more than 100 doctors. Frank was invited to dinner with the family and often told us of how Uncle Paul would carve the turkey with surgical precision. He also visited his grandmother, Laura Bucknell Loyson, but she was not very friendly. France has mandatory conscription for all men to serve in the armed services. Laura called the military police and said he was breaking the law by not serving in the mandatory armed services. They arrested my father but they let him go after he showed them his US passport that did not have his birth name, and he claimed they had the wrong person. My father was so angry and upset at what his grandmother had done he said he would never return to France as long as he lived.

He never did. Upon arriving back to the US with my mom, he legally changed his name and dropped Loyson. He spent the rest of his life as Frank Doster Wetherill.

After my father completed his master's degree at the University of Colorado Boulder, he accepted his first teaching position at Ames High School in Iowa. He enjoyed teaching there and helping with extracurricular activities. He was proud of running the concession stand during football games and often talked about how much money he made for the school.

A few years after teaching in Iowa, he was accepted for his doctoral studies in Romance languages at Pomona College in Los Angeles, California. This is where and when my sister and I were born. A few years later my father's paternal grandmother, Laura Bucknell Loyson passed away. The family tried to disinherit my father again! French law states that the will can only give away 50% of the estate to non-family members and the rest is divided up among the legal heirs. Laura and Paul had three children, Jean, Marthe, and Pauline, and the estate should have been divided up between them equally. The heirs tried to disinherit my father who was due the share of his father, Jean. My father hired a US lawyer who advised him that the way to fight this would be to hire a French lawyer, which would be costly. My father thought that his French family did not have much money because when he visited them, they did not have a nice home and did not even have modern plumbing.

Instead he filed suit in the US courts and one of the other heirs, his aunt Marthe, came to the US to fight the claim. They settled out of court for $10,000 (equivalent to almost $87,000 in 2020 dollars) which he used to further his education and buy a house in California. He also bought two Fiat 500s. My father was wrong about the value of the estate but I can only guess how much a double heiress would be worth! I am sure there are records somewhere in France, but that would take a professional researcher to find this out.

The purchase of his and hers Fiats was a bad idea. One day while driving home from Pomona, a young guy was driving on the wrong side of the road and hit him head-on. My father sustained serious injuries but survived because he was wearing a safety belt. He was in the hospital for about a week because of a head injury caused by hitting his head on the steering wheel. He didn't have a chance against the other driver's big American car. After he recovered, he sold the other Fiat and bought an American Motors Rambler with a fully reclining front passenger seat. He loved this feature since he could fit his model airplanes easily in the car with the seat down. Many teenagers had different uses for the car with the fully reclining seat, which they nicknamed, "Lay-Down Rambler", and the phrase was even used in the Blues Brothers' song, "B Movie Box Car Blues"!

After my father received his PhD in Romance languages, he was expecting to be promoted to a full professorship at Pomona, but wasn't promoted and remained an associate professor. He was upset with this and started to send out resumes to other colleges and universities. He was offered a full professorship at Texas Tech in Lubbock Texas and we moved there in the summer of 1965. He was not happy with the attitude of the redneck school toward foreign languages. My father was a young, aggressive, and proactive teacher. He organized special French and Spanish clubs, along with trips to Mexico for the students to learn by immersion, which was a new and controversial approach at the time. His superiors were very jealous of him and backstabbed him, even trying to send girls to his office to try to get him to change their grades for sexual favors. After three years he got fed up and looked for vacancies at other universities. He then got hired at Ohio Northern University in Ada, Ohio.

This University was better for him, but the infighting among the other professors was vicious. This disturbed and enraged my father. He left after three years and was hired at Thiel College in Greenville, Pennsylvania. It was even worse there, and after two years, he gave up teaching and took a welding course at Tech Memorial High School in Erie, Pennsylvania, not far from Greenville. My sister Carla and I were visiting my mother's parents in The Netherlands that summer, and we did not know that my parents were to move to Erie. This upset my sister more than I, but I was not thrilled, either. It was a difficult time for us. Carla had made many friends in high school in Greenville and didn't get to say good-bye. I was doing well at Penn Middle School and was active in music, playing 1st chair trombone in the 7th grade band. The next year I would have gone to the senior high school and even met with the band director, Mr. Anderson, who was looking forward to my joining the band and stage band. I too left many friends behind.

After finishing his course on welding, my father got hired by General Electric in Erie as a welder on locomotive engines. He worked there for thirteen years and became a union steward. He was good at writing up workers' grievances and had many battles with the company. His nickname there was "The Professor". There were many layoffs and strikes throughout his time there, and during a layoff in 1986 his mother, Dorothy, passed away. He traveled to Denver to help his brother (who was having his own health problems), settle the estate. GE called him to go back to work, but he decided to retire early. He bought a house near LA where my sister lived, so he could be closer to her and his three grandchildren.

He enjoyed his retirement and loved visiting and spoiling his grandchildren. About six years after retiring he had a serious stroke. He had the funds to hire some help to take care of him so he could stay in his house. He had a second stroke about four years after the first one. It left him paralyzed on one side. In 2006 he passed away after he got septicemia from some sores on his feet and he could not recover from the infection.

I learned much from my father. While living in Erie we frequently visited Presque Isle State Park. My father loved to build handmade radio-controlled model boats, and we would sail them on one of the ponds at the park. We had a small inflatable dingy that we strapped to the car roof, if needed, just in case one of the model boats got stranded in the lake. My father told me how to row a boat on these ponds and he told me how he learned to row. When he was a boy he spent some summers with his family at the lodge at Saranac lake which is where he learned to row. This was a favorite pastime of all of the family members including, Emma Bucknell, who also learned to row on this lake. When she escaped the sinking of the Titanic on lifeboat number 8, the male crew members on the raft did not know how to row the lifeboat. She knew how, from her summers at the lodge, and took over one of the oars and helped to row them to safety.

POST LOG

I am writing this in 2020 and 2021. The political climate in the US and world is very disturbed. Many countries, including the US, are becoming more nationalistic and populist. Immigrants are being scapegoated as criminals and leeching off the government. This is a false narrative. The US and many countries have only gotten stronger with the arrival of immigrants, which is why the US is arguably the most powerful and successful country in the world. I am a child of two immigrants. Many of my classmates were 2nd and 3rd generation immigrants from many different countries.

I was exposed to racism as a young boy while living in Texas,. After we moved there in 1965, I sought out friends in my neighborhood. One of the first things they told me is to watch out for the "Mexicans" because they would slash your bicycle seats and tires. Our neighborhood was segregated. The "Mexicans" lived on the other side of town. In 1967 my attitudes started to change. In my school I made friends with a boy who was of Mexican descent. He invited me over to his house to play and meet his family. I accepted and my parents approved. My prejudice was gone. He was just a regular kid from a regular family just like mine!

Erie, Pennsylvania. was a racially mixed city. Many immigrants from Poland, Russia, Ireland, Italy, and descendants of slavery, made up the population. This was a shock for me when we moved there. Greenville, Ada, and even Lubbock were very segregated, and white. In Greenville there was only one black family in the whole town.

In Erie, my first day of school at Gridley Middle School was frightening for me. As I approached the school, there were many black kids arriving and hanging out at the entrance of the school (Erie was about 15% black at that time). As I entered the fear left. Kids were friendly despite their color. My home room teacher was black as were other teachers. My prejudice was gone! My classmates were not racist.

I started taking private trombone lessons at a nearby music store, Markham Music. I went to my first lesson, but had not been previously introduced to the teacher, I only knew his name, Frank T. Williams. I walked downstairs into the basement of the store where the lesson rooms were located. I entered the lesson room and met my teacher, who was a young black man. He quickly won me over and was responsible for me achieving the ability to make music my profession. He is still a mentor of mine and for thousands of his former students around the US. Frank Tecumseh Williams III is a highly respected educator in the US and is now retired from public school teaching, but is still involved in educating kids today.

In the eighth grade at Gridley I was involved in my school music program and had made many friends who were also involved. Towards the end of the year, during band class, a young black man entered the back of the room, very well dressed, and with a perfect afro. He picked up a cowbell and started jamming with the band. Our teacher introduced him as Mr. James Crumbly (aka J.C.), band director of Strong Vincent High School. We were impressed. Most of us in eight and ninth grades would be attending Strong Vincent the next year. He mentioned there would be a summer band camp at Strong Vincent, and wanted to know who was interested in attending the camp. My hand went up as well as those of my friends, and he took our names and contacts. This was a start of a long relationship that continues today. He was a true mentor and inspiration to thousands of students and one of the reasons I am who I am today!

Throughout US history, immigrants have been scapegoated and mischaracterized by the majority who controlled the country, mostly along religious lines. White Protestants were the majority and controlled the country politically. The US was expanding westward with new territories and needed to settle these areas, so they needed to increase the population. The government welcomed new immigrants to expand the workforce.

Anti-immigration started because many people believed that immigrants would steal their jobs. Citizens criticized immigrants' religious and social differences, physical appearance like skin color, and discriminated against them. Each wave of immigrants was scapegoated and discriminated against. Laws like the immigration act of 1924 were enacted to restrict the new arrivals, even though the country needed them to increase the labor force. Slavery was ended after the Civil War and the blacks were also discriminated against. This period in US history, which is referred to as the Jim Crow era, also discriminated against immigrants.

This continues today and is one of the major problems in the US. Discrimination only weakens the country because it divides the nation, does not let all people thrive, reach their potential, and pursue their dreams of a better and more prosperous life. Discrimination and racism concentrates the wealth in the hands of the few and depresses innovation and entrepreneurship.

My father was lucky because he came from a family of wealth and privilege. This helped him become a US citizen, unlike most immigrants who do not have connections in the government. They struggle to find a path to citizenship and if they have entered the county without documentation or overstayed their visas, they live in fear of being deported or jailed. The process to become a US citizen is long, complicated, and expensive. Politicians promise a better path to US citizenship but the path is so steep and so costly that many just give up hope and try to live in the US as best as possible and hope they are never discovered as being undocumented and then deported. They fear that if they try to become US citizens they will be deported and prevented from reentering for years, resulting in being separated from their US families, killed, or imprisoned in their native countries.

The US was populated by many waves of immigrants, each wave making the country stronger, more prosperous, and diverse. There are surges of immigrants from various countries for various reasons including war, poverty, political unrest, climate disasters, and religious persecution. No matter what fears are stoked against immigration, they are completely unfounded and irrational. Anti-immigration laws need to be changed and the path to becoming a US citizen needs to be straightened and accessible to anyone that wants to become a US citizen. Becoming a US citizen may not be the goal for every person that enters the country, and it should not be allowed for every person that wants to become a US citizen. There must be some rules and background checks for this process, but they should not be so difficult and costly to achieve that the process makes it out of reach for qualified applicants. It is my opinion that the anti-immigrant forces have made it hard to become a US citizen because they do not want immigrants to enter the US. They justify forcibly deporting undocumented immigrants.

I don't have all the answers, and no one does, but we need to have discussions about this based on facts and not biased rhetoric. Different cultures are something to be experienced, enjoyed, and encouraged. The US is a diverse country which makes it a better place to live!